Anglican Foundations 12

"Doubt Not...But Earnestly Believe"
A Fresh Look at the *BCP* Baptism service

Mark Pickles

The Latimer Trust

"Doubt Not...But Earnestly Believe" A Fresh Look at the *BCP* Baptism Service © Mark Pickles 2020. All rights reserved.

ISBN 978-1-906327-66-8

Cover photo: 'Little girl on ceremony of child christening in church' by Mylu on AdobeStock.

Published by The Latimer Trust November 2020.

The Latimer Trust (formerly Latimer House, Oxford) is a conservative Evangelical research organisation within the Church of England, whose main aim is to promote the history and theology of Anglicanism as understood by those in the Reformed tradition. Interested readers are welcome to consult its website for further details of its many activities.

The Latimer Trust

London N14 4PS UK

Registered Charity: 1084337

Company Number: 4104465

Web: www.latimertrust.org

E-mail: administrator@latimertrust.org

Views expressed in works published by The Latimer Trust are those of the authors and do not necessarily represent the official position of The Latimer Trust.

COPYRIGHT INFORMATION

Quotations from English Standard Version, The Holy Bible, English Standard Version. ESV® Text Edition: 2016. Copyright © 2001 by Crossway Bibles, a publishing ministry of Good News Publishers.

Contents

Introduction	1
Challenges	2
The Public Baptism of Infants in the BCP	7
Summary Reflection on the Baptism Service	18
The Thirty-Nine Articles and Infant Baptism	22
The Relationship Between the Articles and the Baptism Service	25
Summary Reflections and Suggestions	29

Introduction

At a time when the Christian faith is being increasingly marginalised and the Church of England continues to experience decline, the sacrament of Baptism has come under increasing pressure. As recently as the 1960s, the Church of England still baptised more than half the newborn babies in England and Wales, but this proportion has now fallen to no more than ten percent. Some of this is due to the rapid increase in the number of non-Christian births (mainly Muslim and Hindu), some to secularisation and some to a growing sense that children should be free to choose for themselves and not be baptised as infants when they have no idea what has happened to them.

The 1662 *Book of Common Prayer* sets out a liturgy for infant baptism, which was then the almost universal norm. Although it is little used today, the principles that it lays down are still valid and must form the basis for modern services that seek to remain faithful to the Anglican tradition.

It would be of immense benefit to the ministry and mission of the Church today to have the *BCP* Baptism services, and in particular, the service for the Baptism of Infants, in contemporary language. In this study, I intend to point out some of the challenges that face us in arguing for the provision of such a service, then look in some detail at the theological and biblical principles expressed in the *BCP*, and finally, outline some implications and areas for further consideration.

Challenges

There are several factors, from within and without the church, that mitigate against the need or desire for the provision of a contemporary English Baptism service reflecting a Prayer Book theology.

Decrease in infant baptism[1]

In an increasingly multicultural and secular culture, the demand for and interest in infant baptism continues to decline. The Church of England annually publishes its 'Statistics for Mission' and the 2017 statistics record a further decline:

> In 2007, there was an infant baptism for 14% of live births (and other births will have been followed by later child or mature baptisms) .... In 2017, there was an infant baptism for 10% of live births (and other births are likely to be followed by later child or mature baptisms).[2]

Admittedly, there is considerable variation from one region to another:

> Large variations between dioceses are illustrated by the fact that in 2017 there was an infant baptism for over 25% of live births in Carlisle and Hereford but for under 5% of live births in London and Southwark.[3]

This is not random and arbitrary, but reveals an important trajectory. Cultural influences tend to move from city to countryside, not *vice versa*, so unless there is a dramatic intervention or reversal, the norm for the urban context today will be the norm for a rural context tomorrow.

Use of the Book of Common Prayer

Of those infant baptisms, the vast majority will have been conducted using the *Common Worship* Baptism service. The use of the *BCP* Baptism

---

[1] Church of England Research and Statistics, 'Statistics for Mission 2017', https://www.churchofengland.org/sites/default/files/2018-11/2017StatisticsForMission_007_.pdf.
[2] C of E Research and Statistics 2017, p.15.
[3] C of E Research and Statistics 2017, p.15.

service is rare, particularly in parishes that are mission-minded and intentionally seeking to engage and reach out to their local community with the gospel. A foundational principle of effective evangelism is the need to communicate the gospel as clearly as possible in the language and culture of those you are trying to reach. Elizabethan English does not come naturally to most people in the UK today.

The ironic failure to apply the *BCP* principle

There is an irony here. Many who ignore or abandon the *BCP* on grounds that its language is archaic and culturally obscure are not aware of one of the foundational principles of the *BCP*. On the other side, many who cling to the *BCP* do so because they value its use of language and fear that contemporary liturgies which are written in modern English lack the beauty and richness of the *BCP* language.[4] However, while appreciating the language of the *BCP*, they fail to grasp that the whole point of the *BCP* is to provide a biblically faithful liturgy in the language of those who would use it. Note that the 'C' stands for 'Common' – in other words, available to be used by all, in a language accessible to all! Thus, the Preface to the 1662 *BCP* explains why there have been some changes from previous editions of the Prayer Book:

> Most of the alterations were made ... secondly for the more proper expressing of some words or phrases of ancient usage in terms more suitable to the language of the present times and the clearer explanation of some other words and phrases that were either of doubtful signification or otherwise liable to misconstruction.[5]

---

[4] For example, Prince Charles: 'The vivid and memorable language of the Prayer Book has become part of our Nation's heritage and is, I believe, still vital and necessary to today's life. Yet, over recent years, we have witnessed a concerted effort to devalue the currency of these resonant words. It is hard to escape the suspicion that so many changes have been made to the cadence of the language used just to lower the tone, in the mistaken belief that the rest of us wouldn't get the point if the word of God was a bit over our heads. But the word of God is supposed to be a bit over our heads.' Prayer Book Society, https://www.pbs.org.uk/resources/BCP-350-supporters.
[5] 'Preface', *Book of Common Prayer*, 1662, p.vii.

Aspects of the *BCP* Baptism service are certainly liable to be misunderstood. Although that does not automatically necessitate change, it may warrant further discussion at least. However, it is most definitely the case that there are problems of language that would render the *BCP* Baptism service less accessible for 'present times' and thus hinder its use today, particularly in an increasingly secular age where there is far less residual knowledge of basic Christian doctrine.[6]

Sacramental indifference

The proliferation of various networks, partnerships and training courses has brought many benefits and blessings. Not least, it has helped to re-establish relational trust and fellowship between Anglican evangelicals and their non-conformist brethren which had suffered from tensions going back to the 1960s.

However, the downside of this has been at least an implied downplaying of the significance of ecclesiology, and in particular of the sacraments. Our unity is to be found in a commitment to Biblical authority and the biblical gospel; our differences mainly lie in the area of ecclesiology – our doctrine of the church, church governance and the sacraments. Therefore, to avoid division, there is a tendency either to ignore these subjects or simply to assume the prevailing doctrinal position of the conservative evangelical subculture. This, combined with a chronological snobbery that often leaves us ignorant of our heritage, means that the evangelical atmosphere that we breathe will cause many to imbibe a doctrinal 'credobaptism', almost without realising it.[7] Baptist writers and organisations, like Mark Dever and 9 Marks or John Piper and Desiring God Ministries, are influential among many younger evangelicals. In a 'sacramental vacuum' many will follow them and simply assume that paedobaptism is unbiblical and unhelpful. This is further perpetuated if Anglican clergy are either not convinced paedobaptists themselves or fail to teach their congregation about the value of infant baptism.

---

[6] Anecdotally, a conversation with a jeweller who told of a woman asking for a cross/crucifix: 'I'd like one with that little man on it.'

[7] I use the word 'credobaptism' somewhat reluctantly to distinguish it from 'paedobaptism' – reluctantly in that paedobaptism is also 'credobaptism' but applied differently. Credobaptism: Baptism is only to be administered to those who make a profession of faith.

Furthermore, most conservative evangelicals are committed to expository preaching, working their way systematically through books of the Bible, making it unlikely that they will ever have cause to preach on infant baptism, given that there is no specific New Testament text that either commands or describes it. When, if ever, will many in evangelical Anglican congregations hear a biblical rationale for infant baptism? In addition, the commitment to biblical preaching will attract others who come not because the church is Anglican but because it is evangelical, and many of them will be credobaptist.

As an evangelical Anglican minister, I had the somewhat strange experience of trying to encourage Christian parents who did not want to have their children baptised that they should do so, and of trying to discourage non-Christian parents who *did* want to have their children baptised that they should not!

Memorialism

Again, through lack of explicit teaching, the prevalent understanding of the sacraments among evangelicals is that they are 'bare signs' that point us to spiritual realities and serve to remind us of or to remember the saving work of Christ, but that is all. Their main emphasis is horizontal not vertical and is 'man-wards' not 'God-wards'.[8] This is in contrast to a Roman Catholic *ex opere operato* understanding of the sacraments. Any liturgical pronouncements that appear to convey anything that hints of that Catholic understanding are to be viewed with deep suspicion.[9]

Absence of the Articles

Though the Thirty-Nine Articles are, of course, to be found at the back of the *BCP*, they are noticeable by their absence from *Common Worship*. The consequence is that the Articles have become all but invisible in most churches. Apart from the detrimental impact of effectively side-lining the church's doctrinal confession, the vital and necessary grid for correctly interpreting the *BCP* liturgy, in particular the service for the public baptism of infants, is removed from public view. But, as we shall argue,

---

[8] In other words, the emphasis is on an individual's profession of faith rather than on God's saving activity in Christ.

[9] *Ex opere operato* means 'by the work worked' – the idea that the sacraments automatically convey grace irrespective of the recipient.

the Articles are essential to ensure a right understanding of the liturgy, without which there may be confusion, ambiguity and error.

An indifference to systematic theology

Among some evangelical Anglicans there is an indifference, even a wariness towards systematic theology out of a concern that we might misinterpret the text or impose our 'system' on the text, instead of letting the text speak for itself. Of course that is possible, but such a view is misguided and naive. It is naive because it is impossible for anybody to come to the text 'neutrally'; a prior danger to imposing our system on the text is to be unaware that we have a 'system'.

> Without realising it we read our own ideas into the text. So far as our constantly changing predispositions remain in the background of our unconscious, they remain misleading and dangerous. Our interpretations are inescapably affected by what we bring to the text.[10]

A specific problem this raises for us is that we might assume that we understand what the *BCP* liturgy is claiming when, in fact, our theological illiteracy has led us to make false and hasty assumptions. 'Ignoring heritage is the first step towards heresy.'[11]

These difficulties may be enhanced when we come to look at the content of the service, providing further reasons to ignore the *BCP* Baptism service or simply assign it to the file marked 'irrelevant'. As we turn to examine the content and structure of the service, we will also take note of possible misunderstandings or theological concerns that the text may raise.

---

[10] R. Pratt, *He Gave Us Stories* (Phillipsburg, NJ: Presbyterian and Reformed Publishers, 1990), p.35.
[11] Pratt, *He Gave Us Stories*, p.71.

THE PUBLIC BAPTISM OF INFANTS IN THE *BCP*

The rubric

The rubric at the beginning of the service states that each child to be baptised must have at least three godparents, of whom at least two must be of the same sex as the child. Parents can be godparents provided that there is at least one other godparent. Furthermore, the godparents must themselves have been baptised and confirmed. They are called to fulfil their responsibilities faithfully, which includes the example of 'their own godly living'.[12] The expectation is that the godparents will be professing and active Christians. The minister must also instruct the parents that they bear the same responsibilities as those required of godparents. The rubric also states that no minister is allowed to refuse baptism, but can delay for 'the purpose of preparing or instructing the parents or guardians or godparents'.[13] There is an expectation that preparation and instruction will be given before the baptism takes place.

Minister's declaration

The service begins with an introductory declaration from the minister followed by two prayers, the reading of God's Word, an exhortation from the reading and another prayer. Then the godparents are addressed directly. First, we will consider the opening declaration:

> Dearly beloved, forasmuch as all men are conceived and born in sin and that our Saviour Christ saith, none can enter into the kingdom of God except he be regenerate and born anew of Water and the Holy Ghost: I beseech you to call upon God the Father, through our Lord Jesus Christ, that of his bounteous mercy he will grant to *this Child* that thing which by nature *he* cannot have; that he may be baptised with water and the Holy Ghost and received into Christ's holy church and be made a *lively member* of the same.[14]

---

[12] Public Baptism of Infants rubric, *BCP*, p.263.
[13] *BCP*, p.263.
[14] *BCP*, p.263-264.

These opening words present us with a clear, unequivocal statement of the doctrine of original sin. We are all 'conceived and born in sin', thus allowing no possibility of there being a misconstrued belief in the spiritual 'innocence' of a child, which is the prevalent belief that shapes 'folk religion' today. It naturally follows, therefore, that there can be no salvation apart from spiritual rebirth, 'none can enter into the kingdom of God except he be regenerate'.

Given our human predicament, we are therefore exhorted to pray that God in his great mercy might do what the one being baptised cannot do – namely grant to him the gracious gift of spiritual regeneration. The words 'be made a *lively member'* are in italics, as though to emphasise that true membership of Christ's church is revealed in active participation, not simply by mere profession of faith.

Prayer

This is, at least implicitly, a recognition of our utter dependence upon God in his sovereign grace to show mercy – as opposed to a presumption that the sacrament itself will inevitably be efficacious. As previously mentioned, *ex opere operato* leads to a belief that grace is automatically conveyed by the sacrament. If it is believed that simply through the performance of the sacrament grace is automatically conveyed, there is no need to pray for God to work. The degree that a person believes in the automatic efficacy of a sacrament is inversely proportional to the emphasis he or she puts on prayer, and *vice versa*. It is thus interesting to observe just how great a stress is put on prayer in the Infant Baptism service.

> Almighty and everlasting God, who of thy great mercy didst save Noah and his family in the ark from perishing by water; and also didst safely lead the children of Israel thy people through the Red Sea, figuring thereby thy holy baptism: and by the Baptism of thy well-beloved Son Jesus Christ, in the river Jordan, didst sanctify water to the mystical washing away of sin: We beseech thee, for thine infinite mercies, that thou wilt mercifully look upon *this Child*; wash *him* and sanctify *him* with the Holy Ghost; that *he,* being delivered from thy wrath, may be received into the ark of Christ's Church; and being steadfast in faith, joyful

> through hope and rooted in charity, may so pass the waves of this troublesome world, that finally *he* may come to the land of everlasting life, there to reign with thee world without end, through Jesus Christ our Lord, Amen.[15]

This prayer rehearses God's saving activity in the Old Testament – for Noah and his family through the flood, and the people of Israel through the Red Sea in the Exodus deliverance – and declares them to be a prefiguring of baptism. The baptism of Jesus in the river Jordan makes this connection more explicit, since we see here the use of 'sanctifying' of water for the 'mystical' washing away of sin. The word 'mystical' is important, because it tells us that although water in itself does not wash away sin, it is not a meaningless, empty symbol. In both Noah's and Israel's case, water was something used by God to execute judgment, from which his people needed to be rescued through God's great mercy. So too in baptism, the prayer asks that the child being baptised may be delivered from God's wrath by being received into 'the New Testament ark' – namely, the Church of Christ. The prayer goes on to ask that the child will be kept safe through the 'waves of this troublesome world' and come to the 'land of everlasting life' of which the Promised Land of Canaan is a 'type' or 'figure'.

This prayer affirms the continuity of the Old and New Testament, the need for deliverance from judgment and wrath in both, and God's provision of mercy and grace in both. Although there is no explicit use of the word 'covenant' in the Baptism service, it is clearly set within a covenantal framework, as this prayer makes clear:

> The first actual prayer in the service reminds us of Noah and his family in the ark and of the people of Israel led safely through the Red Sea, so that from the outset a covenant setting is achieved for the administration of the sacrament.[16]

This prayer calls upon God to look mercifully on the one to be baptised and to grant to him all that is being signified in baptism. The washing away of sin, deliverance from God's wrath, membership of Christ's

---

[15] *BCP*, p.263.
[16] John Stott and J. Alec Motyer, *The Anglican Evangelical Doctrine of Infant Baptism*, (London: Latimer Trust, 2008), p.32.

church, and perseverance to eternal life are not automatically bestowed by baptism but, rather, are dependent upon God, which is why the minister 'beseeches' God to act according to his infinite mercies.

Spiritual regeneration

A second prayer continues to call upon God on behalf of the one to be baptised, saying,

> ... We call upon thee for *this infant*, that *he* coming to thy holy baptism may receive remission of *his* sins by spiritual regeneration. Receive *him,* O Lord, as thou has promised by thy well-beloved Son, saying, Ask and ye shall have; seek and ye shall find; knock, and it shall be opened unto you; So give now unto us that ask; let us that seek find; open the gate unto us that knock; that *this infant* may enjoy the everlasting benediction of thy heavenly washing, and may come to the eternal kingdom which thou has promised by Christ our Lord. Amen.[17]

Here there is a sharpening of definition regarding the word 'regenerate'. It is not simply 'regeneration' that is needed, but '*spiritual* regeneration'. There may be an implication of this in the opening words of the service, that speak of the need to be 'regenerate and born anew of water and of the Holy Ghost'; in other words, which to be regenerate and born anew of water alone is insufficient but possible. In other words it would seem that it is possible to be regenerate and born anew of water alone but the one baptised needs not only to be regenerate and born anew of water but also born anew of the Holy Ghost. It is the use of this phrase, more than anything else in the Baptism service, that has and does cause confusion, even suspicion, among evangelical Anglicans. Alongside the archaic language, it is the strongest reason why many would not want to use the service today. We shall return to this matter, as it appears with even greater weight and significance later in the service.

---

[17] *BCP*, p.264-265.

The welcome of Jesus

There then follows a reading from Mark 10:13–16 where Jesus welcomes and blesses children, in contrast to his disciples' attempt to keep the children from him. This serves to place before us not just the welcome of Jesus towards children, but his indignation when they are kept from him – that is not a matter of indifference to Jesus but, rather, warrants a rebuke from him.

This passage presents us with more than just a warm, sentimental picture of Jesus' love for children; it is laden with theological significance. First, it is worth noting the context that can be easily overlooked. Jesus has come to the region of Judea and beyond the Jordan and is on his way to Jerusalem. Therefore the children brought to him are Jewish children, in other words, 'covenantal children'. Contrast this with an earlier incident in Mark 7 when he is in the region of Tyre and Sidon, and there encounters a 'Gentile, a Syrophoenician by birth' (verse 26). When she begs him to cast a demon out of her daughter, Jesus' initial response is, 'Let the children be fed first, for it is not right to take the children's bread and throw it to the dogs' (verse 27). Matthew gives us further detail about this conversation in which Jesus states, 'I was sent only to the lost sheep of the house of Israel' (Matthew 15:24). Her persistence moves Jesus to pity and he grants her request – but the point for our purposes is that Jesus was acutely aware of where and to whom he was ministering.

Jesus took these children in his arms and blessed them. The word 'blessing' can be used in numerous ways in ordinary conversation today, but in the Bible it is a word loaded with meaning and theological significance. It is never simply a casual utterance and especially not from the lips of Jesus. When God makes his covenant with Abram, he promises to bless all the families on earth through Abram. Deuteronomy 27 and 28 pronounce blessings or curses for covenant obedience or disobedience. In Galatians 3:13–14, Paul writes of how Jesus redeemed us from the 'curse of the law' – that is, the judgment and wrath of God – 'by becoming a curse for us', so that in Christ Jesus 'the blessing of Abraham might come to the Gentiles'. Covenant faithfulness brings the blessing, the grace, mercy and favour of God; covenant unfaithfulness or disobedience brings the curse, the wrath and judgment of God. How is it that Jesus could take in his arms and bless young children 'conceived and born in sin'? Only because they were covenant children:

> Obviously this does not apply to all little children ... the statements of our Lord with reference to the membership of infants in the kingdom of God can be applied only to such little children as come within the compass of a covenant situation analogous to that in which our Lord's words were spoken.[18]

> Jesus then takes the children, including infants and blesses them ... blessing is not simply praying for them, it is pronouncing God's name upon them. Blessing is always in the divine name ... Jesus did not baptise the children in water, for the day of Pentecost had not yet come. Those children had received the sign of cleansing already through circumcision. To pronounce the holy name of God upon fallen creatures without a sign of cleansing would not be a blessing at all, for it would call down judgment.[19]

Minister's Exhortation

The minister then applies this text to encourage those bringing infants for baptism to be assured that just as Jesus welcomed children and rebuked those who kept them from him, so too he will now welcome this particular child. That may sound strange to modern evangelical ears. The minister encourages them not only to bring the child to baptism, but also to have great confidence that Jesus will 'embrace *him* with the arms of his mercy; that he will give unto *him* the blessing of eternal life, and make *him* partaker of his everlasting kingdom'.[20] Not only may evangelicals find this strange, but also some may recoil from what may sound like presumption that the sacrament of baptism is automatically efficacious for any who are baptised.

As we shall see, the *BCP* Baptism service does not assume unconditional baptismal regeneration, but it does have a greater confidence in both covenantal expectations for families of believers and the significance of the

---

[18] J. Murray, *Christian Baptism* (Philadelphia, PA: Committee on Christian Education of the Orthodox Presbyterian Church, 1952), p.63.
[19] E. Clowney, *The Church*, (Leicester: Inter-Varsity Press, 1995), p.283.
[20] *BCP*, p.266.

sacrament than many do today. This expectation is both pastorally encouraging but also a stimulus for persevering and expectant prayer. Indiscriminate baptism is harmful not only for those who receive it while making promises that they do not understand or do not believe, but also for believers because it undermines covenantal confidence and expectation.

The exhortation is intended to give us confidence in God's mercy and grace because of all that his Word teaches us about his covenantal faithfulness. It is not surprising that the minister at this point turns once again to prayer: 'Give thy Holy Spirit to *this Infant* that he may be born again be made an heir of everlasting salvation'.[21]

Before we come to the moment of baptism, let us recall what it is that has been impressed most strongly upon the participants in the service: it is the centrality of prayer that God would act in mercy and according to his promises for the individual being brought for baptism. There is an implicit assumption that baptism is not automatically efficacious because if it were, there would be no need to pray for the gift of the Holy Spirit.

Godparents

At this point of the service, the focus of attention shifts to the godparents. However, as John Stott says:

> It is not the godparents who speak for the child so much as the child who is represented as speaking through his sponsors. The child declares his or her repentance, faith and surrender and desire for baptism.[22]

So the godparents are told:

> ...*this infant* must also faithfully, for *his* part, promise by you that are *his* sureties (until *he* come of age to take it upon *himself,*) that *he* will renounce the devil

---

[21] *BCP*, p.266.
[22] Stott and Motyer, *Anglican Evangelical Doctrine of Infant Baptism*, p.19.

and all his works, and constantly believe God's holy Word, and obediently keep his commandments.[23]

It is therefore the infant who promises by 'his sureties', not the godparents who promise. Similarly in the Catechism:

> Question: Why then are infants baptised when by reason of their tender age they cannot perform them [repentance and faith]?
>
> Answer: Because they promise them both by their sureties: which promise, when they come to age, themselves are bound to perform.[24]

Included in what is promised is a commitment to 'constantly believe God's holy Word' which implies a continual exposure to the reading and hearing of God's Word, and an acceptance of its authority in the life of the child as he/she grows. This is further emphasised in the exhortation from the minister to the Godparents after the baptism:

> that *he* may know these things better (the things *he* has promised and professed through his godparents), ye shall call upon *him* to hear sermons and chiefly ye shall provide that *he* may learn the Creed, the Lord's Prayer and the Ten Commandments in the vulgar tongue.[25]

Once again, the expectation is that the child will be continually exposed to the Word of God as it is preached in the local congregation Sunday by Sunday.

Following the renouncing of the devil and his works, the profession of faith and the expression of a desire to be baptised, the minister once again prays for the child, that he or she may die to sin and be raised in Christ.

---

[23] *BCP*, p.267.
[24] *BCP* Catechism, p.295.
[25] *BCP*, p.271.

Consecration of the water

Then, asking that God would hear the prayers of the congregation, the minister prays:

> ... sanctify this Water to the mystical washing away of sin; and grant that *this Child,* now to be baptised therein, may receive the fullness of thy grace[26]

The consecration of the water in baptism was retained by the Anglican Reformers, but they were quite clear that in no sense was it intended to indicate any change in its substance.

> As Cranmer saw it, the baptismal water is indeed holy by reason of the holy use to which it is put. It does not undergo a change in substance but it does undergo a change 'into the proper nature and kind of a sacrament'.[27]

Again the word 'mystical' is used to describe the washing away of sin, alluding to the understanding of the intimate, inseparable connection between the sign and the reality that is signifies.

The baptism

Next, the child is baptised in 'the Name of the Father, and of the Son and of the Holy Ghost', following which, he or she is 'received into the Congregation of Christ's flock' and 'signed with the sign of the cross'.[28]

He or she is then called to confess the faith of Christ crucified and to 'fight' under the banner of Christ against sin, the world and the devil. The fighting metaphor is developed with a call to continue as Christ's faithful 'soldier' and 'servant'.

This metaphor has become quite rare in today's church, partly in a reaction to a wariness of any militaristic language being used or connected with an expression of faith, and partly because it is deemed to be politically incorrect. This is tragic, because it is an entirely biblical theme and one of great importance in Christian living. The minimising or absence

---

[26] *BCP*, p.269.
[27] G. W. Bromiley, *Baptism and the Anglican Reformers* (London: Lutterworth Press, 1953), p.136.
[28] *BCP*, p.269.

of such a theme leaves us unprepared and ill-equipped to live faithful Christian lives in the midst of conflict and opposition. Compare our modern reaction to such a calling with those of our Anglican forefathers, who were only too aware that they were caught up in a cosmic struggle, a struggle that revealed itself in a battle for truth in the church: 'O that we considered often and in deed what we have professed in baptism!' writes Bradford[29] from prison to 'certain godly men'.[30] 'Then the cross and we should be well acquainted together; for we are "baptised into Christ's death"'. He wrote in a similar vein to others when he was awaiting a martyr's death. To Richard Hopkins, Sheriff of Coventry:

> You have professed in baptism to fight under the standard of Captain Christ ... go to, then pay your vow to the Lord; fight like men and valiant under Christ's standard 'take up your cross' and follow your Master, as your brethren Hooper, Rogers, Taylor and Saunders have done ... therefore be not afraid but be content to die for the Lord.[31]

The call to be Christ's faithful soldier comes right at the start of the Christian life and so ought to be one of the self-consciously defining realities for us as we seek to follow Christ. Bradford intentionally connects the call to 'fight' the good fight of faith as a follower of Christ with baptism.

Seeing...that this Child is regenerate

Baptism entails membership into the church, as the one baptised is received into the congregation. That is why, of course, the congregation should be present when the baptism takes place. It is therefore nonsensical to have private baptisms. The minister next declares:

> Seeing now, dearly beloved brethren, that this Child is regenerate and grafted into the body of Christ's Church, let us give thanks unto Almighty God...

---

[29] John Bradford was an English Reformer imprisoned and then burnt at the stake during the reign of Queen Mary.
[30] Philip E. Hughes, *Theology of the English Reformers* (London: Hodder and Stoughton, 1965), p.207
[31] Hughes, *Theology of the English Reformers,* p.207.

Following the Lord's Prayer, the minister continues in prayer for the one baptised, again stating: 'We yield thee hearty thanks ... that it hath pleased thee to regenerate this Infant with thy Holy Spirit'.[32] It may seem at first glance that the plain reading of those words conveys nothing other than a clear belief in baptismal regeneration and we shall return to look at this in more detail. The final exhortation is given to godparents to teach the one baptised the meaning and significance of his baptism.

---

[32] *BCP*, p.270.

Summary reflections on the Baptism service

Prayer

As we have noted, the Baptism service is undergirded by prayer all the way through. Prayer follows the minister's exhortation, prayer follows the reading of Scripture, prayer precedes the baptism, and prayer immediately follows the baptism. This is more than a mere liturgical formality, but rather denotes a prayerful dependence upon the sovereign Lord that the sacrament may be efficacious in the life of the one being baptised.

Gospel

The Baptism service clearly articulates the gospel of grace. It unequivocally states the reality of our 'natural' sinful condition and the need to be delivered from God's judgment and wrath. It understands that the sign of baptism points to death, the washing away of sin through Christ's death on the cross and union with Christ in his death and resurrection.

The Law

In a way that may sound strange to the ears of some modern evangelicals, the Baptism service makes frequent reference to the Ten Commandments, not merely to convict of sin, but primarily as a guide for Christian living. These words are all addressed to the godparents:

> ... this Infant must also faithfully ... and obediently keep his [God's] commandments.[33]

> Wilt thou then obediently keep God's holy will and commandments...?[34]

> ... chiefly ye shall provide that *he* may learn the Creed, the Lord's Prayer and the Ten Commandments ...[35]

---

[33] *BCP*, p.267.
[34] *BCP*, p.268.
[35] *BCP*, p.271.

This is an expression of historic Anglican doctrine as found in the Thirty-Nine Articles, the so-called 'third use' of the law which is an integral part of living a godly Christian life.[36]

Godparents

We have noted that the rubric at the start of the service states that a child must have no fewer than three godparents, but also that parents may be godparents for their own children. On this, Philip Hughes cites Frith:

> Frith rightly warns against the custom of virtually separating the parents from this responsibility (a medieval divorce between nature and grace, which resulted in the parent and particularly the father, being regarded as merely the parent by nature in distinction from the church regarded as the parent by grace). It is an office, he maintains, that 'pertaineth unto their parents, for they are commanded of God to teach their children; so that the parents should be either alone or at least the chiefest, godfathers'.[37]

An awareness of the *BCP* baptism rubric and the medieval historical context helps us to understand how the Baptism service navigates its way carefully between two polarised extremes. Parents are not removed from having the primary responsibility in nurturing the baptised infant in the Christian faith, a vital truth that needs to be continually impressed upon parents today. The primary responsibility for their child's spiritual well-being lies with them and not the church, Sunday School or youth group. This is once again nothing other than covenantal life:

> And these words that I command you today shall be on your heart. You shall teach them diligently to your children, and shall talk of them when you sit in your house, and when you walk by the way, and when you lie down, and when you rise.[38]

---

[36] 'No Christian man whatsoever is free from the obedience of the Commandments which are called Moral' – Article 7 of 39 Articles.
[37] Hughes, *Theology of the English Reformers*, Appendix L.
[38] Deuteronomy 6:6–7.

Paul assumes this continuity in the New Testament, but makes it explicitly clear that the responsibility in this role lies not just with parents, but with fathers in particular. In both Ephesians and Colossians, children are instructed to obey their parents, but the command addressed to parents is in fact addressed solely to fathers.[39]

The other danger is that of divorcing a child's spiritual well-being from that of the church family. Godparents, as representatives of the church family, ensure that there is an explicit connection between baptism and growth in the Christian faith, both taking place within the local church.

Does the *BCP* Baptism service teach baptismal regeneration?

This question arose in the mid-nineteenth century when the then Bishop of Exeter refused to institute George Cornelius Gorham (1787–1857) to the living of Bramptford Speke (Devon), on the grounds that Gorham did not believe in baptismal regeneration. Gorham appealed his case to the ecclesiastical Court of Arches, which ruled in the bishop's favour, and then to the Judicial Committee of the Privy Council, which overturned that judgment in 1850. In the view of the Judicial Committee, the *Book of Common Prayer* must be interpreted by the Thirty-Nine Articles of Religion. The Articles stress that a sacrament is only valid if received by faith, the presence (or absence) of which cannot be determined in the case of an infant. In other words, baptism is not a kind of spiritual vaccination that takes effect, whether the recipient is aware of it or not. Some high-church clergymen became Roman Catholics as a result of this judgment, but the vast majority stayed in the Church of England, and baptismal regeneration has never been official Anglican teaching since then.

The first NEAC (National Evangelical Anglican Congress) at Keele in 1967 produced a Congress Statement that covered liturgical revision. And, as regards the *BCP* Infant Baptism service, it specifically stated:

> In view of the widespread misunderstanding caused by such expressions as 'this child is regenerate' we

---

[39] See Ephesians 6:4, 'Fathers, do not provoke your children to anger' and Colossians 3:21, 'Fathers, do not provoke your children, lest they become discouraged.'

would welcome their revision provided that the covenant basis which they express is not lost.[40]

Would that be the most helpful way forward? Would it be best to remove a phrase that can so easily be misunderstood and that is open to unhelpful interpretations (or, if the intention was to articulate a belief in baptismal regeneration, correctly understood)? For evangelicals, for whom clarity of expression, biblical faithfulness and doctrinal clarity are paramount, the answer would appear to be 'yes', but the matter is not so simple. In what follows, my intention is to explain the *Prayer Book* understanding of baptismal regeneration in contrast to a Roman Catholic understanding. In fact, it is not only the '*Prayer Book* understanding' – it is the commonly agreed understanding among Reformed theologians, Anglican and Presbyterian. My conviction is that, although it is open to misinterpretation (and even more so today with our lack of understanding of sacramental theology), the *BCP* approach is in fact biblical – therefore, the possibility of misinterpretation does not negate its validity or suitability.[41]

---

[40] Keele Congress Statement, 1967.
[41] In Psalm 22:6 David writes, 'But I am a worm and not a man'. He does not say that he is 'like' a worm but that he 'is' a worm. He is thus either lying, being deliberately and unhelpfully ambiguous, or he is, in fact, a quite extraordinarily gifted worm who can not only write in Hebrew, prophesy about the crucifixion of Christ and reign over the nation of Israel. Or he assumes we get the point that he is not talking literally!

The Thirty-Nine Articles and Infant Baptism

This is of vital importance.

The Thirty-Nine Articles are the doctrinal basis of the Church of England

The Thirty-Nine Articles are intended to summarise and to state the doctrinal beliefs of the Church of England. As the Gorham Judgment reminds us:

> The appellant's points, as put by his Counsel, were principally these: The Articles are the Code of Doctrine in the Church of England, the Prayer Book the Code of Devotion. It is not imputed to Mr Gorham that he holds anything inconsistent with the Articles, but that he holds doctrine inconsistent with opinions gathered by the bishop *inferentially* from the Services of the Church.[42]

It was accepted as a valid argument in this test case that the Articles are to be given priority over the liturgy in understanding and interpreting doctrine. Furthermore, the quotation demonstrates that doctrine as stated in the Thirty-Nine Articles is clear, whereas liturgical language can allow for a variety of interpretation by 'inference'.

Anglican doctrine of the sacraments

The Articles set out the Anglican understanding of the sacraments. They clarify that there are only two sacraments, not seven as per the Roman Catholic Church, and that is because they were ordained by Christ in the Gospel. The further distinguishing feature of a sacrament is that it is an outward sign of an invisible grace and that that sign or ceremony has been ordained by God, and thus by inference not the church.

As signs, the sacraments serve as public demonstrations or witnesses of a Christian's profession of faith. However, their greater significance is that they are witnesses and effectual signs of God's grace towards the

---

[42] The Heritage Anglican Network, 11th December 1849, http://theheritageanglicannetwork.blogspot.co.uk/2011/05/gorham-case.html, (emphasis added).

believer. The precise nature of the relationship between the sign and the reality that it signifies is complex and a source of much debate, which we will explore in more detail, with particular reference to baptism. Article 25 gives an introduction to the sacraments in general:

> Article 25: Of the Sacraments
>
> Sacraments ordained of Christ be not only badges or tokens of Christian men's profession, but rather they be certain sure witnesses, and effectual signs of grace, and God's good will towards us, by the which he doth work invisibly in us, and doth not only quicken, but also strengthen and confirm our Faith in him. There are two Sacraments ordained of Christ our Lord in the Gospel, that is to say, Baptism and the Supper of the Lord.[43]

Article 27 then focuses specifically on baptism:

> Baptism is not only a sign of profession, and mark of difference, whereby Christian men are discerned from others that be not christened, but it is also a sign of Regeneration or new Birth, whereby, as by an instrument, they that receive Baptism rightly are grafted into the Church; the promises of forgiveness of sin, and of our adoption to be the sons of God by the Holy Ghost, are visibly signed and sealed; Faith is confirmed, and Grace increased by virtue of prayer unto God. The Baptism of young Children is in any wise to be retained in the Church, as most agreeable with the institution of Christ.[44]

When we turn to the Articles, the possible liturgical ambiguity that we have seen regarding the expression 'seeing that this child is regenerate' is immediately resolved, as the following phrases make clear:

> Sacraments are badges or tokens of a Christian's profession, that is, they publicly mark out those who profess faith in Christ.

---

[43] *BCP*, p.621.
[44] *BCP*, p.622-23.

> They are 'effectual signs of grace ... by the which he doth work invisibly in us and doth not only quicken, but also strengthen and confirm our Faith in him.[45]'

The Articles do not allow us to view the sacraments as 'bare signs'. They are means of grace whereby God strengthens our faith. The popular, maybe even prevalent, view of the sacraments among many conservative evangelicals is that the Lord's Supper is a mere remembrance of Christ's sacrifice made once for all, and that baptism is a sign or a mere symbol of grace, but in no sense conveys it. This is certainly not in line with historic Reformed Anglicanism.

Specifically, as regards baptism, we are told in the *BCP* Baptism service that it is a 'sign of regeneration'. This is perhaps the most crucial sentence of all. Baptism is not regeneration but a *sign* of regeneration, baptism is not the thing itself but *signifies* something else.

They that 'receive Baptism rightly' enjoy all that is signed and sealed by baptism. The Articles in no sense hold an *ex opere operato* view of the sacraments – but the efficacy of the sacrament is conditional on 'true, that is trustful reception'.[46]

---

[45] Article 25 BCP, p.621
[46] W. H. Griffith Thomas, *The Principles of Theology* (London: Church Book Room Press, 1963), p.374.

The relationship between the Articles and the Baptism service

So why then is there an apparent discrepancy between the Articles and the baptismal liturgy? The *Prayer Book* Catechism asks:

> Question: What meanest thou by this word Sacrament?
>
> Answer: I mean an outward and visible sign of an inward and spiritual grace given unto us, ordained by Christ himself, as a means whereby we receive the same and a pledge to assure us thereof.[47]

The nub of the issue is the nature of the relationship between the outward and visible sign and the inward spiritual grace. The Roman Catholic understanding of *ex opere operato* sees such a strong connection between the two that they are thought of as inseparable and indistinguishable; those evangelicals who argue for a 'bare sign' sever all connection between the two. However, the Anglican understanding of the relationship between the sign and the reality signified (nothing other than the historic Reformed understanding) is that of a 'sacramental union'.

Sacramental union

Cranmer and the other English Reformers sought to articulate a Reformed understanding of the sacraments, which was undoubtedly influenced by John Calvin:

> there is in every sacrament, a spiritual relation or sacramental union between the sign and the thing signified: whence it comes to pass that the names and effects of the one are attributed to the other.[48]

The 'signa' and the 'res'

An analogy used to help illustrate the connection between the *signa* (the sign) and the *res* (the thing signified) was that of the hypostatic union[49]

---

[47] *BCP* Catechism, p.294.
[48] *Westminster Confession of Faith* (London: 1646) p.27.
[49] Hypostatic union: the union of the human nature and divine nature in one

of the person of Christ, namely as fully God and fully man, a union without separation or confusion.

> What this means is that, between the sign and the thing signified, the names and effects of the one are attributable to the other ... not because the sign is the thing itself but because of the sacramental union ... just as with the two natures of Christ, so with the relation between baptism and regeneration: there is no conversion, confusion of composition.[50]

Cassidy argues that Calvin makes use of a *duplex loquendi modus*, that is, a 'two-fold way of speaking' concerning the sacraments:

> because of the *duplex loquendi modus* of Scripture ... [he employs] language which is proper of the *res* when speaking of the *signa*. But even in such instances, he makes clear that the sign is not – in fact – the thing signified.[51]

This is telling, not just that Calvin makes use of a *duplex loquendi modus,* but also that it is to be found in Scripture itself. What is significant here, for those who object to liturgical language, for example, that seems to allow for ambiguity and even a sacramental misunderstanding, is that this is precisely how Scripture functions. Those who may be uncomfortable with the declaration 'seeing that this Child is now regenerate' must also wrestle with 1 Peter 3:21, 'Baptism, which corresponds to this now saves you, this not as a removal of dirt from the body but as an appeal to God for a good conscience'.[52]

And consider Titus 3:5: 'he saved us, not because of works done by us in righteousness, but according to his own mercy, by the washing of regeneration and renewal of the Holy Spirit'.

---

person, Jesus Christ.
[50] James J. Cassidy, 'Calvin and Baptism: Baptismal Regeneration or the Duplex Loquendi Modus?', 22 August 2016, http://www.reformation21.org/articles/calvin-and-baptism-baptismal-regeneration-or-the-duplex-loquendi-modus.php.
[51] Cassidy, 'Calvin and Baptism'.
[52] Taken at face value, is Peter really claiming that we are actually saved by baptism, rather than by grace through faith? Surely not!

Or Romans 6:3-4: 'Do you not know that all of us who have been baptised into Christ Jesus were baptised into his death? We were buried therefore with him by baptism into death, in order that, just as Christ was raised from the dead by the glory of the Father, we too might walk in newness of life.'[53]

> This is the strongest word Scripture has to say about baptism and undoubtedly those who stumble at the wording of the *Book of Common Prayer* should long since have stumbled at the words of the apostle ... in a completely unqualified manner, the apostle relates the possession and enjoyment of the benefits of the death and resurrection of Christ to the fact of baptism. Here is complete justification for the statement in the Prayer Book concerning Baptism and Regeneration ... at the very point where even some Anglicans themselves have uneasy consciences, the *Book of Common Prayer* is merely echoing the words and formulations of Holy Scripture.[54]

The wider theological and historical context

The Puritans registered many objections and complaints against the *BCP*, however, what is striking is that relatively few, if any, were to do with the words: 'Seeing that this Child is regenerate'. The Westminster divines viewed baptism as the instrument and occasion of regeneration by the Spirit, of the remission of sins, of ingrafting into Christ (see 28.1). The Confession teaches a form of baptismal regeneration.[55] Robert Letham summarises the various Reformed Confessions as teaching:

> a conjunction between the sign (baptism in water in the name of the Trinity) and the reality (the grace given in Christ, regeneration, cleansing from sin and

---

[53] Note 'all' in verse 3. There is no qualifying word here from Paul – it is not 'some' or 'most' or even 'those who truly believed'.
[54] Stott and Motyer, *Anglican Evangelical Doctrine of Infant Baptism*, p.36.
[55] D. F. Wright, 'Baptism at the Westminster Assembly', in Ligon Duncan, ed., *The Westminster Confession into the 21st Century* (Fearn: Mentor, 2003-2005), vol. I, p. 169, cited in R. Letham, *The Westminster Assembly*, (Phillipsburg, NJ: Presbyterian and Reformed, 2009), p.333.

so on). From this, it is legitimate for the one to be described in terms of the other; this is found in Scripture itself in such expressions as 'baptism saves' (1 Peter 3:21). The divines repeatedly refer to baptism as the 'laver of regeneration' ... the reality is distinct from the sign, yet the sign cannot be detached from the reality, for the two go together.[56]

So, too, Griffith Thomas,

> They [the Reformers] undoubtedly held a doctrine of 'baptismal regeneration', but it was not identical with that of Rome ... they used sacramental language, that is, they employed interchangeably the name of the sign and thing ... this is a well-known principle of Scripture which our Prayer Book follows in speaking of the sign and the thing signified in the same terms ... it may be pointed out that the leading Puritans never objected to the word, 'seeing that this child is now regenerate'.[57]

Evangelical unease concerning the *BCP* wording used in the Baptism service may thus stem from a lack of awareness of our Reformed theological heritage and, more importantly, ignorance of how Scripture itself speaks of the sacrament.

---

[56] Letham, *The Westminster Assembly*, pp.338–39.
[57] Thomas, *Principles of Theology*, pp.383–84.

Summary reflections and suggestions

A contemporary English BCP Baptism service?

I suspect that one of the reasons that there is no contemporary English *BCP* Baptism service in *Common Worship* is that some evangelical Anglicans are not particularly convinced paedobaptists. They are likely to be concerned by the apparent presumption of baptismal regeneration (as it is understood today) and thus have not been too bothered to insist upon the need for a *BCP* service in modern English.

If this is so, it is regrettable. The simplicity of the *Prayer Book* Baptism service is commendable in comparison to the far more elaborate *Common Worship* one. It places great emphasis on the reading of Scripture and the importance of prayer, it gives a clear presentation of the doctrine of original sin (if ever there was a liturgical service in which this needs to be most clearly stated, it is surely the Baptism service), and stresses the necessity of forgiveness and spiritual rebirth.

However, a contemporary English *BCP* Baptism service would need to be more than simply a linguistic revision. The theological and cultural context in which the church ministers and serves today is significantly different from that of 1662 – and baptism, more than the Lord's Supper, must engage very carefully with that cultural disconnect. The *Common Worship* Baptism service reflects this, and there are some elements of that service which merit consideration for a modern *BCP* Baptism service (see 'Missional context for baptism' below).

'Seeing now that this Child is regenerate'?

If there was to be a modern English *BCP* Baptism service, ought this phrase to be removed or retained? There are significant and convincing reasons why it should be removed:

1. For some in the wider church, who employ an indiscriminate baptism policy and who would hold to an *ex opere operato* view of the sacraments, this could appear to give support to such a policy and theology.

2. Our present cultural context is both increasingly secular and, at the same time, more prone to folk religion and superstition. People live quite happily with a smorgasbord of contradictory

beliefs, the less sharply defined the better.[58] A vague belief that some sort of initiatory ceremony for a child would therefore qualify them for 'heaven' if a) the child died, or b) there was such a place with no other requirement other than participation in the ceremony, perfectly suits the spirit of the age. Therefore, it is imperative that there be clarity as to what baptism accomplishes and what it does not, and that people are not offered any kind of false assurance through misunderstanding theological terms being used in the service.

3. For most evangelicals, the phrase is at best ambiguous if not simply wrong or heretical. Although a better understanding of its historical meaning and of sacramental theology would help to clarify and alleviate some concerns, the reality is that that is not our present context. Thus, in all likelihood, it would not be a service that many would want to use.

However, as the Keele Congress Statement helpfully noted, if those particular words were to be removed, it is vital that the covenantal significance of those words should not be lost, and other suitable words should be used in their place. Furthermore, the principle of sacramental union is an important one, indeed a biblical one that has been all but lost or ignored today. And there is a danger that, in seeking to simplify or clarify our terminology, we shall further erode theological literacy. In an ideal

---

[58] 'So what we have now is a country where large numbers of people repudiate religion, but are anyway convinced that there is some form of life after death. What they mean by saying they believe in "life after death" is of course almost impossible to say. But it is at least possible that the growth in a belief in life after death is connected with a declining belief in heaven, or at least hell.' Andrew Brown, 'The Persistence of Superstition in an Irreligious Britain, *The Guardian*, 26 April 2012.
www.theguardian.com/commentisfree/andrewbrown/2012/apr/26/persistence-superstition-irreligious-britain.
Anecdotally, I was asked by a bereaved spouse to conduct the funeral for her deceased husband. She was insistent that she wanted the service in church and that she wanted me as a Christian minister to conduct the ceremony, but she was also insistent that I did not mention the name of Jesus or refer to him in the service. What was striking was that she saw no reason why that might be problematic!

world, it would rather serve as a stimulus to pursue a deeper understanding of sacramental theology... but we do not live in an ideal world.

Covenant theology

Among some evangelical Anglican clergy, confusion about the biblical case for infant baptism – or the lack of clarity about it, or a rejection of it – is often a symptom of deeper malaise, namely a lack of understanding of, or interest in, covenant theology. The Anglican theologian J I Packer, in his booklet *An Introduction to Covenant Theology*, argues for its centrality and significance, claiming that:

> the gospel of God is not properly understood till it is viewed within a covenantal frame ... the reality of God is not properly understood till it is viewed within a covenantal frame[59]

Furthermore, he says that

> the church, the fellowship of believers that the gospel creates, is the community of the covenant, and the preaching of the Word, the practice of pastoral care and discipline, the manifold exercises of worship together, and the administration of baptism and the Lord's supper (corresponding to circumcision and Passover in former days) are all signs, tokens, expressions, and instruments of the covenant, through which covenantal enrichments from God constantly flow to those who believe.[60]

Bold claims – but they demonstrate the unbreakable connection between covenantal theology and paedobaptism.

This side-lining of covenant theology is not a matter of theological speculation, far removed from frontline pastoral and evangelistic matters of everyday life. On the contrary, it is of immense practical relevance to how we bring up and nurture our children in the faith, and how parents are

---

[59] J. I. Packer, 'Introduction', *The Economy of the Covenants between God and Man: Comprehending a Complete Body of Divinity*, (Escondido CA: Herman Witsius, 1990), https://www.monergism.com/introduction-covenant-theology.
[60] Packer, 'Introduction', *The Economy of the Covenants between God and Man*.

to be encouraged and equipped in this great task. The *BCP* Baptism service insists that we not only understand that the children of believers are members of the church through baptism, but also be expectant (though not presumptive) that they will grow up to know, love and follow the Lord Jesus:

> In my experience too many Christian parents are so focused on their responsibility for their children's spiritual lives that their prayers are essentially, 'Lord help me to do my job and fulfil my calling to raise my children in the faith.' They don't stop to listen first to what God has told them about his commitment to our children ... the foundation for what we do for our children is to understand and believe what God has said about his work for them and in them ... Having this confidence in God's faithfulness to his covenant promises is the most important single thing we can do for the salvation of our children. We should pray for them with earnestness but pray with confidence because God has clearly revealed his will for our children and he keeps his promises.[61]

I would suggest that not many evangelical Anglicans would think that having confidence in God's covenant faithfulness is the most important thing they can do for their children's salvation. However, if that is true, it is also wonderfully encouraging and liberating for many parents who are so often filled with a sense of guilt and failure, about of how well they have brought up their children in the faith.

When this is rightly understood, it will also mean that our approach to raising our children in the faith will consist more naturally of nurturing them in the faith rather than subjecting them to an anxious 'crisis-moments' approach, constantly seeking to assess whether they have entrusted their lives to Christ. This is not to deny the genuine need for conversion, or the validity of 'conversion experiences' for those who have been brought up in Christian families. But it is intended to push back against an over-emphasis on this, to the neglect of the healthy and often common experience of Christians growing up in a Christian family, who

---

[61] S. Smallman, *How Our Children Come to Faith* (Phillipsburg, NJ: Presbyterian and Reformed Publishing, 2007), p.15.

cannot give a time or date for when they think they became Christians, but who rather speak of a sense of always having known and loved Christ. This is not only perfectly possible but also a wonderful privilege that need not be apologised for.[62]

Teaching enquirers and the congregation about infant baptism

As always, adequate baptism preparation is of vital importance. This becomes increasingly true in an increasingly secular culture that is less and less Christian. The rubric before the *BCP* Baptism service explains:

> No minister shall refuse or, save for the purposes of preparing or instructing the parents or guardians or godparents, delay to baptise any infant within his cure that is brought to the church to be baptised.[63]

It is imperative that those bringing children for baptism receive thorough preparation, which must entail more than one brief explanatory meeting. To provide proper instruction must, of necessity, entail a full and detailed explanation of the gospel, because baptism is a gospel sacrament. However, by itself, that is not sufficient, because there also needs to be an explanation of baptism's meaning and significance. This must also include a gracious but clear warning of the danger of misusing the sacraments.

Article 25 is of particular significance here. Speaking not just of the Lord's Supper but of both sacraments, it declares that 'they that receive them unworthily purchase to themselves damnation'.[64] This is a missing emphasis today, but it is one that a covenantal background would help us to grasp more fully. Being in covenant with God means that we will receive either covenant blessings or covenant curses. To receive the outward sign without the reality of inward grace is to receive the sacrament in an 'unworthy manner'. If we are not 'in Christ' – that is, united by

---

[62] Again, of course, at some point every Christian has experienced spiritual regeneration, the point is simply that it may not always be clearly known when exactly and that it is perfectly possible that it happened at a very early age. A stronger grasp of covenantal theology would both help us with this, but also enable us to embrace more warmly the theological intent of the *BCP* Baptism service.
[63] *BCP*, p.263.
[64] *BCP*, p.622.

faith, the one upon whom the covenant curse for our disobedience has fallen – then we will ourselves receive the covenant curse for our disobedience. Thus, the imperative need for thorough and adequate preparation because such concepts are unknown and alien in a secular 'post-Christian' culture, and cannot easily be taught without a clear biblical, gospel-framework being in place.

However, the *BCP* rubric also helpfully enables us to avoid an 'overly-scrupulous' assessment of whether or not those requesting baptism truly exercise 'saving faith'. The New Testament is clear (for example, the letter of James) that good works are the evidence of saving faith, but it is also equally clear that baptism is to be administered on the basis of 'profession of faith', *not* on the basis of examined fruit flowing from justification by faith.[65] In Acts 8, Philip baptises the Ethiopian eunuch immediately upon his profession of faith and does not delay in order to test the genuine nature of his profession.[66]

This is important pastorally. The role of the minister is to prepare and explain the gospel, the meaning of baptism and the promises being made, in order that those who enquire of baptism made have true understanding and be able to make an informed decision and an informed profession of faith. Upon that profession of faith, the New Testament encourages us to baptise. The diagram below may help explain the dynamic at work.

Minister: Preparation & Explanation		Parents enquiring about baptism: Understanding & Profession of faith
←	Weight of Responsibility	→

---

[65] For example, 'So also faith by itself, if it does not have works, is dead', James 2:17.
[66] 'See, here is water! What prevents me from being baptised?' Acts 8:36 – not, apparently, a lack of evidence of saving faith attested by good works.

If the minister fails to prepare and explain, and parents make baptism promises and a profession of faith without understanding what they are saying, the minister is culpable for their ignorance and bogus profession. However, if there has been due preparation and explanation and the parents knowingly make bogus promises and commitments the weight of responsibility and culpability is thus transferred to them.

However, not only do we need to teach and prepare those enquiring about baptism, we also need to teach congregations. Some evangelical Anglican congregations are taught little about baptism. For many, their greatest exposure to baptism comes from occasional Baptism services, where a large number of people who do not attend church normally turn up, make promises and professions of faith, have their children baptised and then are not seen again.

While there are many good reasons why expository preaching ought to be the staple diet of our preaching programmes, there is also a vital place for occasional topical preaching, precisely so that certain important doctrinal truths can be addressed more fully. A short series of sermons on baptism, tracing its covenantal significance through the Old Testament and the rite of circumcision, and how that then forms the foundational understanding of baptism in the New Testament, would be extremely beneficial for an Anglican congregation. There are, of course, other ways in which it might be explored more fully – Lent courses, seminars, evening courses or as part of a membership class explaining what it means to be an Anglican church, and so on.

The necessity of human responsibility

The relationship between divine sovereignty and human responsibility is a complex one – one over which much theological ink has been spilt. This impacts our understanding of the sacraments in general and of baptism in particular. The *BCP* Baptism service presents a carefully nuanced integration of the two with the greater emphasis rightly being placed on God's sovereign grace. It does make clear the necessity for a response of faith on the part of the one baptised:

> Wherefore, after this promise made by Christ, this infant must also faithfully, for his part, promise by you that are his sureties, (until he come of age to take it upon himself,) that he will renounce the devil and all

his works, and constantly believe God's holy Word and obediently keep his commandments.[67]

Not only that, but baptism is also in part an expression, an outward sign, of our commitment to Christ, a profession of faith being made before others. This is also given expression in Article 25: 'Sacraments ordained of Christ be not only badges or tokens of Christian men's profession'.[68] But, as the Article implies, that is part of the significance but not the only – indeed not the main – focus or emphasis of the sacraments.

The joy of divine sovereignty

So Article 25 continues, 'but rather they be certain sure witnesses and effectual signs of grace, and God's good will towards us'.[69] The greater emphasis is placed upon God's sovereign grace, to an extent that is stronger than some evangelicals, who place the emphasis in baptism on our profession of faith rather than God's covenant faithfulness, might expect.

Frequently, in teaching about baptism, I will ask those who are married, 'What does the ring on your finger remind you of?' Unfailingly the answer comes back: 'that I am married.' When pressed a little more, a variety of answers are then given: 'It reminds me of love that has no end or beginning,' 'it reminds me of my marriage vows,' 'it reminds me of the promises I made to my wife,' and so on. I continue to press, 'No, what does that ring on your finger remind you of?' Eventually the penny drops: 'Ah, this ring reminds me of the promises my wife made to me!' Precisely, and the ring on her finger is there to remind her of the promises that her husband made to her.

And so too with baptism. It is not primarily about my promises to God but a sign of his promises and commitment to me. Luther's typically colourful account of his response to Satanic attack may well sound strange to evangelicals today, but it demonstrates an ever-present awareness of the ongoing significance of his baptism:

> Devil, rage as much as you please, I do not boast of my good works ... before the Lord at all, nor shall I

---

[67] *BCP*, p.267.
[68] *BCP*, p.621.
[69] *BCP*, p.621.

> despair on account of my sins, but I comfort myself with the fact that Jesus Christ died and rose again ... Therefore, be gone ... If I have committed some sin, go eat dung; it's yours. I'm not worrying about it ... This is not the time for arguing, but for comforting myself with the words that Jesus Christ died and rose for me ... And for a sign of all this I have his dear baptism, his gospel, his Word and sacraments.[70]

For the Reformers, baptism was primarily a declaration of the divine grace with an objective reference. The approach was theocentric. This was the basic cleavage between the Reformers and their Anabaptist opponents.[71]

So the minister gives this exhortation:

> Doubt ye not therefore, but earnestly believe, that he [Jesus] will likewise favourably receive this present infant; the he will embrace *him* with the arms of his mercy; that he will give unto *him* the blessing of eternal life, and make *him* partaker of his everlasting Kingdom. Wherefore we being thus persuaded of the good will of our heavenly Father towards this infant, declared by his Son Jesus Christ ... let us faithfully and devoutly give thanks unto him.[72]

This is not presumption, but rather an expression of wonderful confidence in the sovereign grace of a covenant God.

Missional context for baptism

The most significant difference between the theological and cultural context of the 1662 Baptism service and our twenty-first-century context, is that of the transition from 'Christendom' to a 'post-Christian' culture. Assumptions that are implicit within the *BCP* Baptism service are no longer valid today, thus the Baptism service must reflect the missional context in which the church ministers and serves. We see in the interface

---

[70] M. Luther in J. Pelikan et al., eds, *Luther's Works*, 55 vols (Philadelphia, PA: Fortress Press, 1957-1975), p.241–42.
[71] Bromiley, *Baptism and the Anglican Reformers*, p.111.
[72] *BCP*, p.266.

between baptism and culture, a perfect illustration of the wisdom that is needed in cultural engagement in a missional context today. The church needs to be able to extend a warm, gracious welcome to all who enquire, to seek to establish and develop a strong and loving relationship with those it is seeking to reach and, within that relationship, to present the call of the gospel to repent and believe. It needs both to welcome and to confront.

Therefore, the *BCP* insistence that the minister cannot refuse to baptise any infant is no longer appropriate. Our context has changed. However, the intention behind that prohibition is to be cherished. If there are now conditions in which it would not be appropriate to baptise infants, in other words, where there is no evidence of saving faith, or where there is evidence of a lifestyle that does not reflect biblical norms, in those enquiring, we must not retreat too hastily behind a high wall of disengaged purity.[73] To refuse to baptise anyone who does not come to church or who is not a church member makes baptism policy a lot easier and tidier, but fails to do justice to the call to welcome and engage people for the sake of the gospel.

Delay is allowed for in the rubric for preparing or instructing parents and godparents, but in a missional context this ought to be more explicitly insisted upon. The *BCP* Baptism service does indeed charge the parents and godparents:

> Dost thou, in the name of this Child, renounce the devil and all his works, the vain pomp and glory of the world, with all covetous desires of the same, and the carnal desires of the flesh, so that thou wilt not follow nor be led by them?[74]

However, the *Common Worship* Baptism service is more explicit in not only asking if the parents and godparents have turned from sin and evil, but also whether they have turned to Christ as Saviour and Lord:

---

[73] Unimaginable in the context of 1662 is the complexity of modern family life, with its attempt to redefine marriage or ignore it altogether.
[74] *BCP*, p.267.

The Decision

The president addresses the candidates directly, or through their parents, godparents and sponsors

We all wander far from God and lose our way: Christ comes to find us and welcomes us home. In baptism we respond to his call.

Therefore I ask:

Do you turn away from sin?

I do.

Do you reject evil?

I do.

The candidates, together with their parents, godparents and sponsors, may turn at this point.

Do you turn to Christ as Saviour?

I do.

Do you trust in him as Lord?

I do.[75]

This is a helpful reflection of an attempt to acknowledge and engage with a more missional context. However, it would be even better for this part of the service to have an even more explicit call to repentance and faith in Christ, according to the biblical gospel.

Although the number of those enquiring for baptism has declined, it is still one of the great gospel opportunities that local Anglican churches have to share the gospel with members of its community. When those within our parishes, for whatever reason, make the effort to contact their local church with a request for baptism, it is of paramount importance that they receive a warm and gracious welcome and response. If the local church is to be enabled to respond to that enquiry, not only by welcoming warmly, but also by explaining, teaching and sharing the gospel, it needs

---

[75] *Common Worship* Baptism service (London: Church House Publishing, 2000).

to be equipped with a biblically clear and theologically robust Baptism service.

However, it is not just for evangelistic purposes that we need to have biblical faithful Baptism service in contemporary English, but also for the edification of the congregation.

In the Old Testament, the institution of the Passover meal was expressly for the purpose of instruction:

> And when your children say to you, 'What do you mean by this service?' you shall say, 'It is the sacrifice of the Lord's Passover, for he passed over the houses of the people of Israel in Egypt, when he struck the Egyptians but spared our houses.' (Exodus 12:26–27)

Baptism services also provide the opportunity for instruction for those who have been baptised, to remind them again of God's covenant promises to them, the significance of their own baptism and, above all, to declare God's great act of salvation in the life, death, resurrection and ascension of our Lord Jesus Christ.

A contemporary *BCP* Baptism service would provide ministers and local churches with a biblically faithful explanation and presentation of the gospel through the sacrament of baptism.

The Anglican Foundations Series

The Anglican Foundations series is a collection of books which offer practical guidance on Church of England services in the Book of Common Prayer.

These include:
- The Faith We Confess – An exposition of the Thirty-Nine Articles
- The 'Very Pure Word of God – The Book of Common Prayer as a model of biblical liturgy
- Dearly Beloved – Building God's people through morning and evening prayer
- Day by Day – The rhythm of the Bible in the Book of Common Prayer
- The Supper – Cranmer and Communion
- A Fruitful Exhortation – A guide to the Homilies
- Instruction in the Way of the Lord – A guide to the catechism
- Till Death Do Us Part – "The solemnization of Matrimony" in the Book of Common Prayer
- Sure and Certain Hope – Death and burial
- The Athanasian Creed
- The Anglican Ordinal
- "Doubt Not...But Earnestly Believe" – A Fresh Look at the BCP Bapstism Service

The Anglican Ordinal: Gospel Priorities for Church of England Ministry by *Andrew Atherstone*

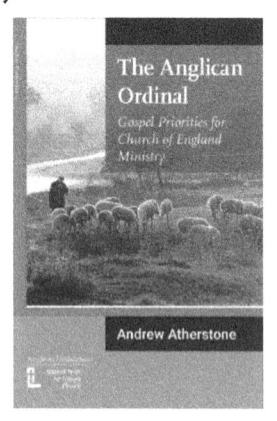

This book is part of our *Anglican Foundations* series, which offers practical guidance on Church of England services.

There is no better handbook for Anglican ministry than the Anglican ordinal – the authorized liturgy for ordaining new ministers. The ordinal contains a beautiful, succinct description of theological priorities and ministry models for today's Church. This booklet offers a simple exposition of the ordinal's primary themes. Anglican clergy are called to public ministry as messengers, sentinels, stewards, and shepherds. They are asked searching questions and they make solemn promises. The Holy Spirit's anointing is invoked upon their ministries, with the laying-on-of-hands, and they are given a Bible as the visual symbol of their new pastoral and preaching office. This booklet is a handy primer for ordinands and clergy, and all those responsible for their selection, training, and deployment.

OTHER RECOMMENDATIONS

Thomas Cranmer: Using the Bible to Evangelize the Nation by *Peter Adam*

We need not only to do evangelism, but also to develop contemporary gospel strategies which we trust, under God, will be effective. We need gospel wisdom, as well as gospel work. We need to work on local evangelism, but also work on God's global gospel plan. This alerts us to our own nation, as well as other nations. Gospel strategy includes the question, 'How should we evangelise our nation?' Thomas Cranmer, Archbishop of Canterbury 1532-56, strategised and worked to do this from the perspective of Anglican Reformed theology and practice. We cannot duplicate his plan in detail, but he can inspire us, and also teach us the key ingredients of such a plan.

His context of ministry had advantages and disadvantages! Our context has the same mixture. We can also learn from Cranmer's ability to work effectively in his context, despite the many problems, and the suffering he endured. God used him to evangelise his nation at his time. May God use us for his gospel glory!

Focus on Jesus: A Guide to the Message of Handel's Messiah by *Robert Bashford*

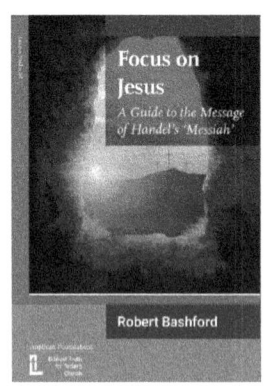

This book provides a commentary on the message of *Messiah*. Handel's great oratorio gives a marvellous portrayal of the Person and Work of Jesus Christ: the anticipation of his coming, his birth, his ministry, his sufferings and death, his resurrection and his ascension – plus also the proclamation of the Gospel to the world, and Christian assurance of resurrection life beyond death.

The main focus of this study is the selection of Bible verses that make up the work, compiled by the librettist Charles Jennens. At the same time there is also a certain amount of comment on the music, showing how Handel's distinctive skill contributes towards clearly expressing the message.

The aim of the book is that readers may deepen their understanding of the Bible passages included in the work, and enjoy Handel's *Messiah* all the more – and as a result know Christ better.

Come, Let Us Sing: A Call to Musical Reformation by *Robert S. Smith*

Come, Let Us Sing seeks to help us reform the musical dimension of church life by bringing biblical clarity to two key questions: Why do we come together? and Why do we sing together?

In answer to the first, Robert Smith navigates a path through the contemporary 'worship word wars', concluding that we gather both to worship God and to encourage others. Two questions must, therefore, be asked of everything we do: Does it glorify God? and Does it edify others?

As to why we sing, Smith unpacks three principal functions of congregational singing in Scripture – as a way of praising, a way of praying and a way of preaching. In so doing, he explores the necessity of singing scriptural truth, the value of psalmody, the place of emotions, the role of our bodies, and how singing expresses and enriches our unity.

Come, Let Us Sing is a timely call for the church to reclaim its biblical musical heritage and reform its musical practice.

Lightning Source UK Ltd.
Milton Keynes UK
UKHW011826250221
379303UK00001B/11